The Jewish Position on Other Religions

The Jewish Position
on Other Religions

by

SINA COHEN

"What is hateful to you, do not do to your fellow human; this is the whole Torah. All the rest is a commentary to this law; go and learn it."

—The Talmud (Tractate Shabbat 30-31a)

S. Research Publications
London • Los Angeles

10 9 8 7 6 5 4 3 2 **1**

A catalogue record for this book is available from the British Library
USA Library of Congress Control Number: 2013943001
ISBN: 978-0-9576744-0-0

To the righteous of the Nations,
Jews and non-Jews alike.

RECOMMENDATION & PRAISE

"Interfaith relations should be based on respect and not on dialogue. But at a time when some religious leaders malign other faiths it is important to have a brief and accurate explanation of all major religions. Sina Cohen has done this clearly, fairly and concisely."

- **Rabbi Dr. Abraham Levy OBE**
    Spiritual Head, Emeritus. Spanish and Portuguese Jews' Congregations, United Kingdom

"Classical Jewish philosophy sees little virtue, actually, in studying other religions — not because they are all completely false, but because among monotheistic religions there are many paths to the top of the mountain and Jews ought to remain on their path — and other monotheists on their own path. But little is gained by looking at a different path than the one you are actually on. It is clear, however, that works like this volume for college students are needed in our current times as many of the youth in our community are considering other paths from the ones their ancestors joyously walked down. In such an environment, the study of other faiths might be needed to reaffirm the value of one's own. This fine work by Sina Cohen fulfills that purpose and its author should be praised for addressing the needs of his community in such a well written way."

- **Rabbi Dr. Michael Broyde**
    Dayan Beth Din of America
    Professor of Law, Emory University School of Law

"*The Jewish Position on Other Religions* is no doubt a summary of the main ideas of the three monotheistic religions in a concise form as partly observed in the Jewish sources, and for somebody who has no idea, or little knowledge of them, this book is a vivid introduction which calls for further investigation."

- **Professor Moshe Sharon**
    Professor of Islamic History, The Hebrew University of Jerusalem

"In addition to studying our own religion, it is of great importance that we invest in learning about other religions to understand the boundaries but also the possibilities for shared learning, collaboration, and pluralism. Sina Cohen's work moves us forward in the right direction and he should be commended for advancing our great Jewish tradition's approaches to the other."

- **Rabbi Dr. Shmuly Yanklowitz**
    Founder & President of Uri L'Tzedek, Orthodox Social Justice

"This book enables us to look at another faith through an Orthodox Jewish lens. Thankfully, we live in a society where we have a right to be equal as well as different. The Psalmist wrote, *"Grant me understanding that I might live."* If we are to live with one another, we must learn about each other. Sina Cohen helps us take this necessary step forward in a most respectful manner."

- **Rabbi Joseph Potasnik**
    Executive Vice President, New York Board of Rabbis

"I believe that Sina Cohen's work, *The Jewish Position on Other Religions,* is a very useful and concise compendium which puts into the hands of Jewish students (or even their non-Jewish interlocutors) essential knowledge about Judaism as well as where and why we differ from other faiths."

- **Rabbi Rashi Simon**
  Founding Director, Kesher

"Sina Cohen's book is well researched and well organized. In my work as a Rabbi I frequently encounter young people who are searching for answers to the very questions that this book addresses. The book will serve as a great resource to both Jewish and non-Jewish people seeking to learn more about Judaism and its relationship with other religions."

- **Rabbi Jonathan Gross**
  Senior Rabbi, Rabbinical Council of America

"Sina Cohen has written a most helpful guide to a topic that is commonly misunderstood – Jewish approaches to other faiths. He offers a thorough coverage of traditional sources and presents the material in an ordered and systematic way, allowing the untrained reader access to a clear statement of Jewish beliefs and doctrines. Mr. Cohen is to be commended for his efforts — I am confident that this work will be an important tool for young Jews to better understand the underpinnings of their religion and deepen their commitment to it."

- **Rabbi Dr. Harvey Belovski**
  Rabbi of Golders Green Synagogue, United Kingdom

"Sina Cohen's book, *The Jewish Position on Other Religions,* is an important, well-written, well-researched and timely book. He deals cogently and succinctly yet sensitively with the major differences between Judaism and other major religions in a vital effort to bring clarity to these discussions. This compact book should be required reading for all Jews that wonder about the beliefs and interact with peoples of other faiths. It is especially critical for Jewish college students who are bombarded with and seduced by the allure of other faiths, while their own precious heritage has not been fully explored. I recommend this book wholeheartedly."

- **Rabbi Ben-Tzion Spitz**
  Chief Rabbi of Uruguay

"We finally have a concise book that Jews, especially students, can refer to when their religion is challenged by adherents of other faiths. It is an indispensable book that deserves a place on the shelves of both Jewish and non-Jewish students around the world. Sina Cohen portrays a very interesting and vital insight into the Jewish responses to other faiths, in a language that even readers who are new to the topic could understand and absorb."

- **Rabbi Daniel Mechanic**
  Founder & Director, Project Chazon

"I congratulate Sina Cohen for preparing this most concise and valuable work which can enable young Jews everywhere to have ready answers when challenged by missionaries on campus or off."

- **Rabbi Yitzchak Rosenbaum**
  Associate Director, Emeritus. National Jewish Outreach Program

GLOSSARY

THE HEBREW SCRIPTURES (also "the Old Testament." Hebrew: "TaNaKh") — These are the Holy Scriptures of Judaism and consist of three segments: The Torah, The Book of Prophets, and The Writings. These Scriptures are considered by Judaism, by Christianity and by Islam as of Divine origin.

THE TORAH — This is the first of the three main sections of the Hebrew Scriptures, and is the Law of God as dictated by God to the prophet Moses. Also known as The Five Books of Moses.

THE BOOK OF PROPHETS (Hebrew: "Nevi'im") — This is the second part of the Hebrew Scriptures in which, besides the various prophecies, the history of the Jewish People and its development as a nation in its land is told.

THE WRITINGS (Hebrew: "Ketuvim") — This is the third part of the Hebrew Scriptures and includes some more of the historical narrative continued from the Book of Prophets. The Writings include the Psalms, Proverbs and the Five Scrolls.

THE TALMUD (also "Jewish Tradition") — This is the body of Jewish civil, religious and ritual law and incorporates the text (the Mishnah) and the ensuing debates and discussions (the Gemara) of the great teachers in the academies in the land of Israel and Babylon and includes also the deep insights and allegories of the greatest Rabbis, legends, folklore and folk wisdom.

THE CHRISTIAN SCRIPTURES (also "The Christian Bible") — This contains the Old Testament and the New Testament.

THE OLD TESTAMENT — This is a Christian term referring to the Hebrew Scriptures.

THE NEW TESTAMENT — This is the second part of the Christian Scriptures, which records the life and teachings of Jesus and his disciples.

THE QURAN — This book consists of the sacred writings of Islam believed by Muslims to be revealed by God to the prophet Muhammad through the angel Gabriel.

THE HADITH — This is a collection of traditions containing the sayings and teachings of the Islamic prophet Muhammad. Hadith are regarded by traditional Islamic schools of jurisprudence as important tools for understanding the Quran.

ISRAELITES (also "Hebrews") — The archaic name for the ancestors of who are known today as the Jewish People.

MONOTHEISM — This is the doctrine or belief that there is only one God.

POLYTHEISM — This is the doctrine or belief that there are many gods.

ACKNOWLEDGEMENTS

I am forever indebted to my Father, the first author I ever met, for teaching me the most liberating of faculties — to question. "Thank you" to my kind yet brutally honest Mother who zealously played the role of devil's advocate during many religious debates with me.

Thank you to all the Rabbis, Priests, Imams and other religious leaders that I have had the pleasure of meeting and studying with in England, Israel and the United States. I appreciate your sitting down with me to patiently explain your arguments, whilst listening to mine.

I would also like to show my appreciation to all the notable individuals who have reviewed this book and provided it with recommendations and approvals. Specifically, special thanks must be given to my teacher and friend, Rabbi Osher Baddiel of London, England. Your input has provided this book with much life and character, and I wholeheartedly appreciate your time and dedication to the cause.

Finally, a big thank you must be reserved for the old lady that knocked on my door as a Jehovah's Witness when I was only 15 years old. You provided me with the very first encounter I had with somebody who challenged the very foundations of my religious beliefs, and spurred me on to seek the truth.

CONTENTS

"Study subjects through which you will be able to answer the heretics and non-believers should they question you."

— Moses Maimonides (Perush HaMishnayot)

"Be diligent in the study of Scripture; and know what answer to give the non-believer."

— Rabbi Elazar ben Azariah (Pirkei Avot 2:19)

"Even though the study of those matters needed to reply to the non-believer may appear to be of a non-obligatory nature, it is nevertheless esteemed by God as equal to the study of the Torah and the performance of the Mitzvot (commandments)."

— Rabbi Samuel d'Ozeda (Midrash Shemuel)

PREFACE

This book was inspired by the Jewish student.

Why don't Jews believe in Jesus?

Why don't Jews follow the Quran?

What makes Judaism different to other religions?

It is very likely that you have been confronted with at least one of the questions above or have at least pondered them.

All through my university days as a student in England, my religious faith was constantly challenged. My search for the answers began as I delved into the study of comparative religions and compared the various tenets each faith-system proudly upholds.

I took pleasure in reading the Islamic Hadiths, the medieval commentaries of the Christians, and the wisdom of the Jewish Pirkei Avot as much as I enjoyed discussing the teachings of the Buddhist Sutras and the mantras in the Hindu Rigveda. There was just so much to learn, and the parallels between the faiths were clear to me - but make no mistake about it, so too were the differences. I and those around me have always tried to reconcile these differences, these "contradictions", and we try to explain them as being different shades of the same colour.

Nevertheless, I have always asked myself, *why did my Jewish ancestors not accept the claims of other religions? What was the status quo before many of the later religions came about?*

Today, with zealous missionaries and preachers trying to convert us by giving speeches on our university campuses, and even occasionally on our doorsteps, the reality on the ground forces us to intellectually "hold our own" and properly address these questions. This is why I decided to address this important topic.

After years of debating with eager fellow students, studying with a variety of religious leaders and diligently analysing many diverse religious texts, I have attempted to compile and summarise the claims that have been made by others together with the answers to the questions that many of you have — or will soon — come across.

The book begins with a short introduction to Judaism. This is followed by an analysis, from the Jewish perspective, concerning the religions of non-Jews. But the crux of this book will be the Jewish **response** to fellow monotheistic faiths — Christianity and Islam. This book also includes some discussion concerning other religions such as Hinduism and Buddhism.

There is a considerable effort by certain groups within other religions to actively convert Jews – this book is a short response to them. In no way does this book intend any disrespect to other religions and faiths. Rather, I intend to clarify why Jews have remained Jews throughout history.

"All religions that came after the Torah of Moses are part of the process of bringing humanity closer to the essence of Judaism, even though they appear its opposite.

When the Messiah arrives, all nations will become one tree, recognising the common root they come from and which they had previously scorned."

— **Rabbi Yehuda HaLevi (The Kuzari 4:23)**

INTRODUCTION

There is no single Jewish position on other religions. Jewish tradition has produced a variety of views, ranging from the benevolent and tolerant, to the dismissive.

It is hardly unsurprising that historically, those Jewish views of non-Jews and their religions which are least tolerant have generally been held by Jews who experienced oppression by non-Jews at the time. Conversely, many of the accepting and tolerant views tend to be held by those Jews in places where Judaism was allowed to exist and thrive.

But historical events and their effects aside, Judaism has always held that even if non-Jewish people do not subscribe to the religious practices or beliefs of Judaism, so long as they were decent people abiding by the moral values of humanity, they deserved to be respected as human beings and with a part to play in God's world. Indeed, Judaism teaches that all righteous people have a portion in the World to Come.

WHY WE STAND WHERE WE STAND

Without challenges to our Jewishness, we tend to become quite comfortable in our surroundings and take refuge in the security of our religious circle without really knowing why we believe what we believe and why we do what we do. However, challenges do arise and that is why it is imperative that we should understand what it is that we believe and why we do what we do.

However, it is equally important to be aware of what it is that we **do** **not** believe, and **why**, or else misunderstandings will grow in our minds. This will lead to an inability to respond to the questioners and indeed this has been the concern of some of our great Jewish leaders and thinkers.[1]

Judaism is the first monotheistic religion in the world and it has faced many challenges, often the most brazen challenges from the very sects that derived their teachings from Judaism. Many of these groups later attempted to convert the Jewish People to their ways and this is the position today, too. So it is important for Jewish people to learn and to know why we did not surrender nor give in to their threatening claims; to know how to counter their arguments and respectfully disagree.

Looking back through Jewish history, we see that the minds of many of the great Jewish leaders, at the same time as probing and understanding the depths of Judaism, were also aware of the claims that other religions made against Judaism and they often stated why we do not accept them. These leaders ably contended with the most heretical of opinions.[2] They were often forced against their will to debate with virulent and vicious opponents[3] and they invariably won — even when the rules of debate were skewed against

---

[1] E. Erlbach, E. Glucksman, P. Forsccheimer, B. Elliot, *The Living Hirschian Legacy.* (Feldheim, K'hal Adath Jeshurun, 1989), pg. 98-101
[2] The Talmud — Sanhedrin 39a; Avodah Zarah 16b—17a; Hagigah 5b
[3] E.g. The Barcelona Disputation, The Tortosa Disputation, The Paris Disputation

them. Today, there seems to be a loss of conviction, probably brought about by a lack of knowledge and this has sadly led to some Jews losing their way and leaving the Jewish People. There is no doubt that a lack of knowledge of Judaism and of what it means to be Jewish, and if we do not know **why** we stand where we stand, will have a detrimental effect on future generations. For that reason, we must have our response ready. This book is part of that response.

JUDAISM AND THE CHALLENGE OF THE NEW

Any change in a *status quo* needs to be justified. If people are happy in their religious conviction and satisfied that it is correct and good but someone comes along to change the situation by introducing a new belief or a different way of life, the newcomer will have to justify his changes. If someone sets out to challenge a long-standing religious teaching and way of life by claiming to be a prophet with a new message, it is obvious that we thoroughly examine his credentials and his new message.

It is a matter of historical fact that Judaism and the Jewish People were in existence for at least two thousand years before anybody else made their claims of prophecy. Prophecy first arose amongst the ancient Hebrews, the ancestors of the Jewish People, and the Torah[4] and Jewish tradition[5] provide definitive and clear

---

[4] The Torah — Deuteronomy 4:2, 13:1—4, 18:17—20
[5] Moses Maimonides, *Mishneh Torah*. Hilchot Yesodei HaTorah, Chapters 7—10

criteria of who can and who cannot be a prophet for the Jewish People. The Jewish People therefore know who can be a prophet for them and who cannot. Anyone who rises up claiming to be a prophet sent by God to change the original established law and religion cannot be a prophet for the Jewish People.[4] This does not mean that God does not send prophets to relay messages to non-Jewish people – the story of the prophet Jonah is just one example that proves otherwise.[6]

The problem today is that many people are not aware that Judaism existed for a long time before any of the later religions, who attempted to change the *status quo* (that is, Judaism), emerged. People are not aware that the dominant religions of today are in fact relative late-comers and that, although many individuals attempted to convince the Jew to abandon his laws for theirs, the Jew did not waver.

But first of all, we need to be aware of the situation that existed before the newcomers sought to change things. This will help to explain why the Jewish People never yielded to the noisy and often violent calls shouted at them down the ages for them to give up their heritage, their religion and their cherished way of life.

---

[6] The Book of Prophets — Book of Jonah

WHAT IS PROPHECY?

Prophecy is the means that God uses to communicate to mankind and thus guide human society along the path of righteousness and good. A prophet may receive a call to prophesise for a number of reasons:

1. To remind us of our responsibilities and duties and to warn us of the consequences if we should wander off the path that God intends for us.

2. To foretell the future when God deems it necessary that we should be aware of what is to come in order to encourage us in our mission in life.

3. To deliver private messages to a particular individual, *i.e.* an important individual whose actions are liable to have a widespread effect.

A prophecy will never contradict or annul an earlier commandment from God.[4] Since God has warned us in the Hebrew Scriptures that He does not cancel His previous prophecies, it follows that **a person claiming that God has told him to change the way of life that God has commanded, thereby disqualifies himself as being a prophet for the Jewish People.**

For Jews, a prophet is not meant to start a new religion.[5] He comes only to encourage us to follow the Torah, warning people not to violate its laws. Indeed, the last words of prophecy ever spoken are, *"Remember the Torah of Moses my servant."* [7]

---

[7] The Book of Prophets — Malachi 3:22

שְׁמַע יִשְׂרָאֵל יְהֹוָה אֱלֹהֵינוּ יְהֹוָה אֶחָד

Hear, O Israel: God is our Lord,
He is the One and Only One.

— The Torah (Deuteronomy 6:4)

1 – WHAT IS JUDAISM?

Judaism is the oldest monotheistic religion in the world. It is the fountain of faith in God from which Christianity and Islam took their inspiration. Judaism is the foundation stone upon which are built the moral values acknowledged as correct throughout the world. Just think about it, many of the basic ethical ideas and the true moral principles of Western civilisation are based upon the Ten Commandments of the Hebrew Scriptures.

JUDAISM & MORALITY

Many historians have noted the significant influence that Jewish ethics have had on true moral behaviour throughout the ages, down to today.[1]

The Greeks contributed to the world much of the arts and philosophy. The Persians spread throughout the world astrology and poetry. The Romans brought to the world government and a degree of democracy and the Chinese invented paper and gunpowder.

But the fact is that these nations, as indeed all the nations of the civilised ancient world, perpetuated and even praised practices and values that today are universally acknowledged to be barbaric, cruel and repugnant to any civilised person.

---

[1] W.A. Irwin (1947) *The Intellectual Adventure of Ancient Man: An Essay on Speculative Thought in the Ancient Near East.*

Today, if you dispose of your unwanted babies or old folk by abandoning them in the freezing outdoors (like the ancient Greeks) or use minors for sexual relations and watch humans kill each other simply for entertainment (like the ancient Romans) and generally ignore the feelings and rights of those that are less privileged than you, it would be recognised as wrong and would not be tolerated. Yet these things were done unashamedly in the so-called civilised societies of the ancient world.

The ethics and morality of Judaism was entirely different. Judaism preached and practiced kindness and generosity and care for the underprivileged and the helpless. Yet for their noble teachings and ethics which were so different to everybody else's, the Jews were denigrated and insulted by almost every nation of the world who all called Judaism crazy, bizarre and radically out of touch with everybody else.

But in the end, and as the nations of the world slowly learned from the Jews to behave humanely, considerately and morally, this Jewish ethic became the acknowledged standard for humanity.

So, where did Judaism all start?

ABRAHAM, THE FATHER OF MONOTHEISM

Judaism started approximately 4000 years ago (16th century BCE) with a man named Abraham who was born in Mesopotamia.[2] The culture and the religions of the peoples of Mesopotamia and surrounding regions at that time were polytheistic. The people worshipped all kinds of idols and they believed in a multitude of gods. Abraham was a seeker, a person of superior intelligence and of great intellectual integrity and he questioned and challenged the polytheistic culture of his time. He came to the conclusion that all of existence comes from a single Source — a single non-corporeal and infinite God. Abraham is recognised as the father of Judaism because of his discovery of this most fundamental tenet of Jewish faith.

Abraham set it as his life's task to teach others his belief in the one God and the consequences of this great truth. For many years and without any word from God that he was right in his chosen way of life, he carried out his self-appointed mission, fearlessly defying powerful priests and despotic kings, to teach the world about the one God. Only when Abraham was seventy years old did God appear to Abraham for the first time and He then bestowed upon him His blessing that his descendants will eventually grow into a nation that will perpetuate all that he believes in. Later, God promised to Abraham that his descendants will inherit the land then occupied by the Canaanites as a part of this covenant between God and His nation, the Jewish People.[3]

---

[2] Ancient Mesopotamia is modern Iraq, but also parts of eastern Syria, southwest Iran, and southeast Turkey.
[3] The Torah — Genesis 12:1. Modern-day Israel makes up most of this region.

Abraham passed on his belief and his teachings to the son born to him from his wife Sarah, Isaac (and to Ishmael, born to him fourteen years earlier from Sarah's handmaiden, Hagar), who in turn passed these teachings and mission to Isaac's son Jacob (later also called "Israel"). Jacob faithfully passed on this belief in God and the teachings of Abraham to his twelve sons, whose families grew into the twelve Tribes of Israel.

FROM THE DEPTHS OF EGYPT TO THE HEIGHT OF MOUNT SINAI

Abraham obeyed the command of God to travel away from his father's house and from the land of his birth to the land at that time inhabited by the Canaanites.

In 1522 BCE, this land (Land of Canaan) suffered a severe famine which forced Jacob and all of his sons and their families to temporarily move down to Egypt. They were invited by Pharaoh, the king of Egypt, to stay as honoured guests (Joseph, Jacob's son, had saved Egypt from a terrible famine) but eventually they were enslaved by the Egyptians and they had to endure bitter slavery. But they never lost faith that God would deliver them from their slavery and after more than two hundred years they had grown from a family group of seventy souls into a Hebrew nation of some two million people, still faithfully maintaining their belief in God, preserved and passed down from their ancestor Abraham.

This Hebrew nation was led out from Egypt by the prophet Moses who was chosen by God to lead them, firstly, to Mount Sinai in the wilderness to receive there the Ten Commandments and the rest of God's commandments to His people, and then to go on from there to the land promised by God to the Children of Israel, the descendants of Abraham, Isaac and Jacob.

And so, on their way through the wilderness to the Promised Land, they came, as had been arranged and foretold, to the foot of Mount Sinai. There, God revealed Himself to the entire nation in a National Revelation that has never been repeated in all the history of the world as He gave them His law, called the Torah (the word "Torah" means "instruction") which was to guide the Jewish People, that is, the Hebrews, until today and forever.[4] Those laws that all the people heard from God Himself at Sinai are called the Ten Commandments.

LIVING IN THE NATIONAL HOMELAND

After forty years of travelling in the wilderness, the Hebrew people finally came into the Land of Israel under the leadership of Joshua, the successor of Moses. They established a period of over twelve hundred years authority of the Land, with worship of the one God focused around the Temple in Jerusalem.

---

[4] "The Torah" — meant here are the Five Books of Moses. Later, the Book of Prophets and the Writings formed altogether the 24 books of the Hebrew Scriptures, called **TaNaK**h, an acrostic formed from the initial letters of **T**orah, **N**evi'im [Prophets] and **K**etuvim [Writings]. This is all of holy writ and is called by the term "Old Testament" by the Christians.

EXILE AND RETURN

The Jewish People sinned by deserting the Torah and God punished them by allowing the country to be conquered by the enemies of the Jewish People and the First Temple was destroyed by the Babylonians in 586 BCE. There was a return to the land and the Temple in Jerusalem was rebuilt. For some centuries the Jewish nation dwelled in their land but they neglected the Torah and they sinned again and so it came about that the Second Temple was destroyed by the Romans approximately 500 years later. The war and occupation of the land by the Romans with their cruel casting out of the Jews from their country into slavery and banishment resulted in the long Jewish exile. The majority of the Jewish nation was widely dispersed throughout the Roman Empire and eventually even beyond that, too. Many Jews were dragged down with the Roman conquerors to Spain, Italy and to all the countries that lay along the coast of the Mediterranean (these later became known as "Sephardi" Jews) as well as in central and northern Europe (these later became known as "Ashkenazi" Jews).

This exile of the Jews, dispersed all over the world, has lasted for more than 2000 years. All through this time, Jews always prayed three times a day that God should return them to their Holy Land and this dream started to be fulfilled in 1948 CE when a majority vote in the United Nations allowed the re-establishment of a Jewish State in the land of Israel — in the same land which was promised by God to Abraham and his descendants all those centuries before.

But whether they are on their land or off it, as the people of the Torah, the Jews are duty bound to be God's "Chosen People" and, as such, the influential moral force in the world.[5] Contrary to popular misconception, the Jews are not "chosen" to be a superior race.[6] As stated above, the Torah teaches that all humankind is precious to God and mankind is the crown of creation. Each folk group, each nation, has its place in God's plan and has its purpose and role in the world. The Jewish People's role is specifically to teach all of mankind of the existence of God.

God promised Abraham that his descendants will be blessed and that the world will be blessed through his children[7], and viewing the Jewish contribution to society and civilisation one can clearly see how this promise is continually fulfilled.

---

[5] The Torah — Genesis 17:7; Exodus 19:5—6; Deuteronomy 7:7—8, 14:12
[6] The Kuzari — 1:92-103, 2:35-44
[7] The Torah — Genesis 22:17

FAITH

Jews believe in:

o   The one God
o   The Hebrew Scriptures
o   The prophets in the Hebrew Scriptures

WAY OF LIFE

Judaism is based upon:

o   The Commandments in Hebrew Scriptures, including:
   o   Prayer and devotion only to the one God
   o   Dietary rules ("Kosher")
   o   Observance of the weekly Sabbath and holy days
   o   Moral relations between male and female
   o   Righteousness in social relations
   o   Dress and other symbols

THE JEWISH PEOPLE

o   A people united by a common heritage and mission to bring Godliness and morality to all mankind, a "light unto the nations" *(Isaiah 49:6)*
o   Currently over 16 million all over the world

"Ask now about the days of long ago, long before your time, ask about the day that God created human beings on the earth, ask from the end of the heavens to the other – ask this: Has anything as great as this national revelation at Mount Sinai ever happened, or has anything like it ever been heard of? Have any other people heard the voice of God, as you have heard it, and lived?"

— The Torah (Deuteronomy 4:32)

2 – JEWISH BELIEF & NATIONAL REVELATION

Just take a look at the many, many religions of history, and you will notice how almost all of them have one thing in common: they were started by individuals who attempted to convince people that he or she have been sent by God to pass on a message. However, for Jews, this has always been a difficult concept to grasp.

After all, there was no one else who heard or who was there to see God speak or interact with this person so everybody has to take his word for it. Even if the individual claiming to be a messenger of God performs miracles, these miracles do not necessarily prove that he is telling the truth: he might be a magician or something. So even being able to perform 'miracles' merely shows that the claimant has certain powers — it does not prove their claims to be true. In fact, the Torah states that God sometimes grants the power of 'miracles' to individuals, in order to test the loyalty of the people to God.[1] Furthermore, from the Torah itself we can see that not all 'miracles' are works of God: in the account of the Exodus, the magicians of Pharaoh's court were able to imitate some of the miracles that Moses and Aaron did.[2]

---

[1] The Torah — Deuteronomy 13:4—5
[2] The Torah — Exodus 7:11

On the other hand, there is Judaism. Unique among all of the world's major religions, Judaism does not rely on any individual's claim of any revelation nor does it rely on any miracles as the basis for its authenticity.

It is only Judaism that has as its foundation, not belief in one individual and his vision or prophecy, but real live Divine Revelation to the whole assembled Hebrew nation. That is, God spoke to the entire people — a National Revelation.

Come to think of it, this makes good sense, too. After all, if God wants to introduce a new set of laws to mankind, it doesn't make sense to just let one or two people know about it. It's only right that His entire nation should hear it, and so indeed it was. The Torah was given to Moses, with all of the Jewish People as witnesses to the Divine Revelation, and this is an unequivocal fact that both Christians[3] and Muslims[4] accept. The Torah states clearly that there were 600,000 men[5] at the Revelation at Mount Sinai. In addition, there were their wives, their children and the elderly as well as a great number — *"the mixed multitude"* [6] — of Egyptians and others who came out of Egypt with them. At a conservative estimate there were more than two and a half million witnesses of the revelation who stood

---

[3] The Christian Scriptures includes the Old Testament, which is merely a Christian term for 'the Hebrew Scriptures,' and thus includes an account of the events reported in the Torah, including the Revelation at Sinai.
[4] The Quran — 2:63, 5:44, 6:91, 17:2
[5] The Torah — Exodus 12:37
[6] The Torah — Exodus 12:38

at Mount Sinai. This is in stark contrast to many other world religions, as follows:

Christianity   An individual named Paul is on the road to Damascus and experiences a revelation in which Jesus of Nazareth, who at that time had already been dead for over five years, appears to him and tells him his life story. Paul immediately converts to Christianity (that is, to follow the teachings of Jesus) and goes back to preach the word of Jesus to the world. This is the beginning of Christianity.

Islam   An individual named Muhammad meditates alone inside a cave on Mount Hira and the angel Gabriel appears to him. Muhammad then indirectly receives a series of messages from God which are later gathered into chapters to form the Quran, the main Islamic holy book. Muhammad goes on to preach what he has experienced to others.

Buddhism   An individual named Siddartha Gautama settles down alone under a Bodhi tree where his soul ascends to heaven and he achieves enlightenment and becomes a *Buddha.* His soul returns into his body so he is able to spread among mankind the knowledge that he gained during his spiritual experience.

This recurring model, where one or two individuals experience a revelation of sorts on their own and then manage to convince others, is the pattern of the beginnings of almost every world religion — but not Judaism.

Through comparative religious study, one could deduce that no leaders or holy men of any religion are able to show any evidence for their claims of authenticity the same as Judaism can show the truth of its origin and its scriptures. Most of the founders of other religions refer to future events or to later worlds or they make only vague statements that are not very provable in this world. The Hebrew Scriptures, however, are full of very specific information and prophecies of future events, in this world.

So how can we prove that National Revelation actually occurred?

If the accounts by numerous individuals are all broadly identical, if they are generally accepted by everybody and they all describe clearly what occurred, then the story must be true. There is no way that an account of an event in the past should be in the collective memory of a people had these factors not been present at the time of that event.

For example, unless they actually occurred, one cannot hope to convince a whole crowd of people that explosions took place at the Eiffel Tower in France at a given time last week — unless they had actually happened. There are simply too many witnesses who were there and who know that it's a lie. The story would never be accepted as true and certainly would not be recorded as an event in history other than as an attempted hoax.

We know that there was a French Revolution, and that Napoleon was defeated at Waterloo, simply because the events were witnessed by large numbers of people. Individuals can make things up and might convince even a large number of people to believe them but it will always be an event started by an individual. If a great number of people all together pretended that an event occurred but in fact it hadn't, then there will always be others who will stand up and vigorously dispute the claim.

It is crucial to note that the major religions actually testify to the truth of the revelation at Mount Sinai in their own scriptures. They all acknowledge this revelation at Mount Sinai as the only one where the one God revealed Himself to an entire nation.

The great Jewish philosopher Maimonides[7] states[8]:

> *The basis of Jewish belief is the Revelation at Mount Sinai, which we saw with our own eyes and heard with our own ears, not dependent on the testimony of others ... as it says in the Torah in Deuteronomy, "Face to face, God spoke with you" and "God did not make this Covenant with our fathers, but with us — who are all here alive today."*

Judaism does not simply rely on the account of any miracles by an individual, however great and however

---

[7] Moses Maimonides (1135—1204) was a preeminent medieval Spanish, Jewish philosopher and physician, and one of the most prolific and widely-accepted codifiers of Jewish law.

[8] Moses Maimonides, *Mishneh Torah.* Hilchot Yesodei HaTorah Chapter 8

trustworthy that individual might be. The truth of Judaism is confirmed by the personal experience witnessed by every man, woman and child, standing at Mount Sinai over 3000 years ago.

And don't forget: the Jewish People are not a nation of sheep! They are probably one of the most skeptic people in the world! It's not easy to pull the wool over *their* eyes!

"The righteous among all the nations of the world will have a share in the World to Come."

— **The Talmud (Sanhedrin 105a)**

3 – NON-JEWISH PEOPLE

Even only a cursory study of comparative religions soon reveals that different religions make very different claims. Many do so in a definitive manner without leaving much room for religious pluralism.[1] Almost every religion — except Judaism — claims that it is the exclusive source of all truth, the fount of all wisdom, and that everybody else must accept these truths or be damned. All outsiders, according to many other religions, need to be saved from this damnation by being converted to "the religion of truth." Judaism, on the other hand, unlike any of the major religions of the world, does not see its mission to actively convert anybody. In other words, you don't have to be Jewish to get into heaven! This is called religious pluralism and it is almost unique to Judaism.

It is important to distinguish between religious pluralism and religious tolerance. Religious tolerance means peaceful co-existence between adherents of different religions despite very different beliefs and practices — something that many religions today have come to adopt due mainly to changes in society's religious standards (and "political correctness"). Religious pluralism, however, goes a step further than religious tolerance, for religious pluralism recognises that other

---

[1] Religious pluralism: A view that holds that there can be commendable values and some level of truth in other religions as well as in one's own religion.

peoples may have other beliefs and gives validation to these people's other beliefs. Judaism teaches religious pluralism and this is one of the reasons why Judaism stands out from other world religions.

JUDAISM & RELIGIOUS PLURALISM

Just take a look at the calendar systems of major religions such as Christianity and Islam and you may conclude that they reflect an exclusionary philosophy; each begins with the birth of their respective religion. On the other hand, the Jewish calendar begins with the creation of Adam, the first human being, teaching every Jewish boy and girl the intrinsic value of each human being, even though the Jewish religion was not yet born at the time of Adam. Furthermore, we are taught in the first chapter of the Torah that the animals and the plants were all created *"according to their various kinds"* [2], but that human beings were created without any such differences. All humans are of the same kind. Judaism emphasises the intrinsic value of each and every human being, that regardless of their colour of skin or any other racial differences, all are created in the image of God. Jew or non-Jew, there is no difference in their humanity.

Traditionally, Jews believe that God forged a unique covenant with the Jewish People at Mount Sinai. This gave the Jewish People a particular goal — to be a *"light unto the nations"* [3] — and the responsibility to spread

---

[2] The Torah – Genesis 1:24—28
[3] The Book of Prophets — Isaiah 42:6, 49:6, 60:3

the moral message to all of mankind. This belief, however, does not prevent the idea that God has a relationship with other peoples, as Judaism believes that God entered into a covenant with **all** of humanity at creation. Judaism's most cherished ideal is that of the universal brotherhood of mankind.[4] This can clearly be seen, for instance, from the fact that there are non-Jewish prophets[5], and how Moses referred to God as the *"God of the spirits of all flesh"*.[6]

However, Judaism does not demand anyone but Jews to adhere to the 613 commandments of the Torah, since it is the Jews who inherited this obligation from their ancestors when they stood at the foot of Mount Sinai. There is, however, the clear duty upon all human beings to live by basic moral guidelines. According to Jewish tradition[7], these guiding principles come in the form of seven laws that were given by God to Adam and his wife Eve, the first human beings, for all humanity.

These laws are called the Seven Noahide Laws because after the Great Flood all of humanity is descended from Noah and his family.[8] Any non-Jew, belonging to any folk or nationality, belonging to any race or any people, who lives his or her life according to these Seven Noahide Laws[9] commanded by God, is considered as

---

[4] B. Drachman, *19 Letters of Ben Uzziel.* (New York, 1942), pg. 15

[5] The Talmud — Baba Bathra 15

[6] The Torah — Numbers 27:16

[7] The Talmud — Sanhedrin 56a—60a

[8] The Torah — Genesis 10:32

[9] These Noahide laws are based on Chapter 9 of Genesis, the first section of the Torah.

"righteous" and is assured of a place in the World to Come.

THE SEVEN NOAHIDE LAWS

1. **Do not worship idols.**
2. **The law against blasphemy.**
3. **Do not murder or unlawfully inflict pain on any human.**
4. **Do not steal or deal dishonestly in trade.**
5. **The law against incest and sexual immorality.**
6. **The prohibition to eat the flesh torn from a living creature or to cause any unnecessary pain to any living creature.**
7. **To establish institutions of law and order and justice and the upholding and enforcing of these Seven Noahide Laws.**

These laws point to a decent, moral and humane society that reflects the way that God desires all people to live together.[10]

Are Christians, Muslims and adherents of other religions also bound by these Seven Noahide Laws?

Despite the differences in religious belief and practice, Jewish law most certainly acknowledges other religions as long as the basic moral conduct of humanity, rooted in these Seven Noahide Laws, is part of these religions.

---

[10] Benamozegh, *Israel & Humanity.* pg. 237-259

The Chief Rabbi Emeritus of the UK, Lord Rabbi Dr Jonathan Sacks, sums up the general Jewish answer[11]:

> As Jews we believe that God has made a covenant with a singular people, but that does not exclude the possibility of other peoples, cultures, and faiths finding their own relationship with God within the shared frame of Noahide law.

This does not mean that we should be blind to the important on-going debate between religions. In the words[12] of Rabbi Irving Greenberg, one of the greatest advocates of Jewish Pluralism, *"It is just that those disagreements are for the sake of Heaven. In other words, part of pluralism is that you don't necessarily reconcile or come to agreement. But you do understand the validity and role of the other, even when they disagree."*

Even though there might be various religions, the ultimate destination, namely, coming close to God and serving Him, is the same. It is mainly only the paths to that destination that is different.

•

"The Lord is good to all, and His mercy is upon all His works."
- The Writings, Psalm 145:9

"[The Prophet Elijah said]: I call heaven and earth to bear witness that anyone – Israelite or gentile, man or woman, slave or handmaid – if his deeds are worthy, the Divine Spirit will rest upon him."
- Seder Eliyahu Rabba 9:1

---

[11] J. Sacks, *The Dignity of Difference: How to Avoid the Clash of Civilizations.* (London, New York: Continuum, 2002), pg. 55

[12] A. Chasan, "Disagreeing in the Service of God." *Rabbi Irving on Jewish—Christian Relations.* Beliefnet, Mar. 2006. Web. 17 Jan. 2013.

4 – CHRISTIANITY & JESUS

What is Christianity and who was Jesus?

Christianity arrived on the world scene over 1300 years after Judaism. It began as a Jewish sect which evolved into a separate religion. It is based on the life and teachings of Jesus of Nazareth, also known as Jesus Christ (the word "christ" comes from the Greek "christos," meaning "anointed," which in turn is the translation of the Hebrew word "Mashi'ach", hence "Messiah."). He was a Jewish disciple of one of the great Rabbis in ancient Israel in the first century CE. The Christians say that he was conceived by his mother without any biological father and this is the credo of "the virgin birth."[1] He is considered by many Christian denominations as the awaited Messiah foretold in the Hebrew Scriptures[2], called by some "the son of God,"[3] and by others is considered as God in human form.[4]

The Roman oppressors who had overrun the land of Israel considered him a rebel against their authority (he called himself *"the king of the Jews"* [5]) and they killed him by their normal method of execution, crucifixion.

---

[1] The New Testament — Matthew 1:18; Luke 1:26—35
[2] The New Testament — Mark 8:29; John 4:25—26, 8:24, 8:58; Matthew 16:16
[3] The New Testament — Matthew 16:15—17; John 10:36, 20:31; Luke 22:70
[4] The New Testament — 1 Timothy 3:16
[5] The New Testament — Mark 15:26; Luke 23:38; Matthew 27:37; John 19:19—20

Christians say that after his crucifixion, Jesus was later resurrected and came back to teach his followers how to live their lives. The accounts of Jesus' death and his resurrection were later written down over the next years and decades by his followers in their various versions and these different accounts of episodes in the life of Jesus and his teachings are known today as the "New Testament."

What is the Christian position on Judaism?

Christians include the Hebrew Scriptures in their collection of holy books, and collectively refer to them as the "Old Testament." However, the "New Testament" claims that Jews did not obey the words of the Hebrew Scriptures[6] and that the arrival of Jesus as the Messiah has rendered the original Jewish covenant with God invalid. The New Testament goes on to state that Christianity is thus the fulfilment and successor of Judaism.[7]

This traditional Christian position on Judaism is called "Replacement Theology" or "Supersessionism." This means that God has unilaterally abolished the covenants that he had originally made with the Jewish People, and instead had made a new covenant with the Christians — even though the Hebrew Scriptures themselves state unequivocally that *"[the Torah] applies to us and our*

---

[6] The New Testament – Acts 7:51—53
[7] The New Testament – Hebrews 7:11—28, 8:6—13

children forever" and that the covenants will never be cancelled.[8]

Jesus and all of his twelve disciples (except Luke) were Jewish and Jesus is portrayed in the New Testament as obeying certain Jewish laws: he defends Rabbinic authority[9]; he attends Jewish festivals[10]; and even wears tassels[11] as prescribed in the Torah.[12]   Nevertheless, considering his claim to *"uphold the law and not to abrogate it"* [9], it is hard to comprehend how he disobeyed many other fundamental Jewish laws such as those associated with the Sabbath and Kashrut (dietary laws).

Christianity highlights the importance of believers to spread the message of Jesus Christ ("the Gospel") from *"house to house"* [13] and all over the world.   Christian preachers of this message are encouraged and exhorted in the New Testament to specifically target Jews[14], to use any methods to get Jews to accept Christianity, with the conversion of a Jew being the top prize in the task of bringing the message to the unbelievers of the world. This preaching and converting is called "evangelism."

---

[8] The Torah — Deuteronomy 29:28. Also see ibid. 13:1, 32, 33:4; Leviticus 23:14, 26:42—44; The Writings — Psalms 12:6—7, 119:152, 119:160

[9] The New Testament — Matthew 5:17—19

[10] The New Testament – Mark 6; 1 Corinthians 11:24; John 10:23—30; Matthew 17:24—27

[11] The New Testament — Mark 6:56, Matthew 14:36

[12] The Torah — Deuteronomy 22:12, Numbers 15:37—39

[13] The New Testament — Matthew 7:6, 10:11, 24:14, 28:18

[14] The New Testament — Romans 11:25—26; John 4:22; Matthew 23:39; Ephesians 3:6; Romans 1:16

Indeed, Jesus himself states that he will not return until the Jewish people accept him as their Messiah and convert to his ways.[15]

The great eagerness and effort to convert non-Christians is due to the Christian doctrine that salvation and entry to heaven relies **only** upon the belief in Jesus Christ as the Son of God and the Messiah.[16]

The following words from Jesus himself demonstrate clearly the Christian position concerning non-Christians:

"I [Jesus] am the way, the truth, and the life.
No one comes to the Father [God] except through me."

– The New Testament, John 14:6

For many centuries, the Jews have faced severe consequences for their rejection of Jesus as the Messiah. Historically, Jews have been under constant persecution by Christians who were influenced by certain passages of the New Testament.[17]

What is the Jewish position on Christianity?

Due to the various denominations of Christianity, a thorough analysis of the particular group is required before a specific conclusion can be made and thus there is no single Jewish approach to Christianity. Additionally, a Jewish source that discusses Christianity may be referring to a specific Christian sect with a specific

---

[15] The New Testament — Matthew 23:37—39
[16] The New Testament — Acts 4:12; Timothy 2:5; Romans 10:1—4; John 3:15—16, 3:36, 4:14, 5:11, 5:24, 6:35, 6:51, 8:12, 8:24, 10:9, 11:25
[17] The New Testament — John 8:44; 1 Thessalonians 2:15; Matthew 27:25

doctrine of the particular era in which the source is derived from.

But as far as Jewish law is concerned, the Jewish view as it is reflected in Jewish law ranges between those Jewish Authorities[18] who consider Christianity generally as an outright idolatrous religion and those Jewish Authorities[19] who do not view Christianity as an idolatrous religion but as a "partnership," asserting that Christians (specifically those outside of the Holy Land of Israel[20]) are not true idolaters and that although it is not recommended, non-Jews are not prohibited a "partnership." That is, they permit non-Jews to worship God "in partnership" with another power, imagined or real, human or otherwise, so long as acknowledgement is made of God as the supreme God of gods. Many Jewish Authorities consider the Christian Trinity[21] as such a "partnership", which in Jewish legal terms is called "Shittuf".

---

[18] Moses Maimonides (Mishneh Torah, Hilkhot Avodah Zarah 1:3, 9:4); R. Avraham Eisenstadt (Pithei Teshuva, Yoreh De'ah 147:2); Hazon Ish (Yoreh De'ah 62:19); Hatam Sofer (Responsa of the Hatam Sofer, part A, Orah Hayyim 84).

[19] Menachem Meiri (Bet HaBehirah, Commentary on Avodah Zarah 2b and 6b); Rabbenu Tam (Tosafot to Avodah Zarah 2a; Tosafot to Sanhedrin 63b); Bet Yosef (Bet Yosef, Yoreh De'ah 147; Hoshen Mishpat 182; Shach Yoreh De'ah 151:7); R. Moses Isserles (Darkhei Moshe, Yoreh De'ah 156); R. Yehuda Ashkenazi (Shulchan Aruch, Yoreh De'ah 151:2); R. Judah Asad (Teshuvot Mahri Asad, Yoreh De'ah, no. 170).

[20] The Talmud — Hulin 13b

[21] The Christian Trinity is the Christian Godhead as one God in three persons: Father, Son, and Holy Spirit. This is in stark contrast to Jewish doctrine found in the Torah, Deuteronomy 6:4.

It should be borne in mind that there are some Jewish Authorities who question whether a "partnership" is a permitted form of worship for any non-Jews at all. In practical terms, stringency or leniency might perhaps depend on the standard of religious sophistication of the individual non-Jew.

In any case, "partnership" is prohibited to Jews. This means that Jews are forbidden to believe in the Trinity or to be involved in any form of Christian worship.

Jewish law prohibits any commerce with pure idolaters prior to their holidays[22], so the branding of Christianity as a "partnership" absolves Jews from this restriction. Even so, some Jewish Authorities forbid Jews to visit Christian churches[23], due to the fact that they include images and statues of Jesus and these are considered as idols.

Most kinds of Christians teach that the Hebrew Scriptures have been superseded and that their laws no longer need to be kept, and that the Jews have been replaced by the Christians in the covenant with God. Since the Torah itself says that its teachings are eternal and that its laws will forever remain valid[8], obviously Jews cannot accept these Christian claims and are considered as heresy.

---

[22] The Mishnah — Avodah Zarah 1:1. Jewish jurists did not want Jews to conduct business with idolaters before their holidays lest the money was used for sacrifices, or lest the follower would physically worship his or her idols in gratitude for the business.

[23] The Talmud — Avodah Zarah 17a; R. Jacob Ettlinger (Teshuvot Binyan Zion, no. 63); H. Falk. (1982) *Journal of Ecumenical Studies: "Rabbi Jacob Emden's Views on Christianity"*. 19:1, pg. 105-111

It is worthy of note that there are some Jewish commentators[24] who consider modern-day Christianity as a belief which in some ways is actually contrary to the teachings of Jesus. Rabbis of different eras have regularly distinguished between the teachings of Jesus, whom some regard positively as a sincere teacher, and the later Christian religion and theology that emerged under the influence of the Roman Empire.

The Jewish consensus on Jesus personally is that he is one in a long list of failed claimants, Jewish and non-Jewish, to be the Messiah.

Jews do not accept Jesus as their Messiah, and did not take Christianity as their successor, for a number of reasons, including:

1. ***Aspects of Christianity dispute Judaism***
2. ***Jesus did not fulfil the Messianic prophecies***
3. ***Jesus did not fit the criteria of being the Messiah***
4. ***Verses in Hebrew Scriptures said to refer to Jesus are mistranslations***
5. ***Jewish belief is based upon National Revelation***

First of all, it is important to differentiate between the Jewish understanding of "Messiah" and the "Messiah" of the Christians. Although Christians may think they are the same thing, nevertheless the meaning of the word is actually very different in each faith. Christians believe that their Messiah, Jesus of Nazareth, died for the sins of the people. So according to Christian tradition, the

---

[24] R. Ben-Shalom, *Facing Christian Culture* (Ben-Zvi Institute, 2006), pg. 147—208; Benamozegh, *Israel & Humanity.* pg. 239

Messiah is supposed to be a type of human offering, a blood sacrifice necessary for the forgiveness of sin.

This is in stark contrast to what the Torah clearly teaches in a number of places[25] notably, for instance:

"The fathers shall not be put to death for the children; neither shall the children be put to death for the fathers: every man shall be put to death for his own sin."

- The Torah, Deuteronomy 24:16

Judaism is clear – nobody can die for the sins of others.

---

[25] The Torah — Leviticus 18:21, Deuteronomy 12:31, 20:2—5; The Book of Prophets — Jeremiah 32:34—35

1. Aspects of Christianity dispute Judaism

In the Hebrew Scriptures, God states that all of His commandments will forever remain binding[26], and that the arrival of the Messiah will usher in a period of worldly recognition and acceptance of the laws of the Hebrew Scriptures. Therefore, anyone coming to change these laws immediately identifies himself as a false prophet.[27]

Christians claim that since God made a "New Covenant" with Jesus, the previous laws are no longer binding.[28] They go on to claim that the laws of the "Old Covenant," as commanded in the Hebrew Scriptures (that is, in the Old Testament) were abolished and the laws of the "New Covenant," as laid out in the "New Testament," superseded the laws of Hebrew Scripture when Jesus was crucified.[29]

Furthermore, if the Christian claim is correct that the laws of the original covenant no longer need to be obeyed, then wouldn't it make sense for God to cancel His original commands in the same manner that He gave them? — i.e. in front of all the people, as opposed to supposedly passing on the message of cancellation to one individual?[30]

---

[26] The Torah — Leviticus 18:21, Deuteronomy 12:31, 20:2—5; The Book of Prophets — Jeremiah 32:34—35
[27] The Torah — Deuteronomy 13:1—4
[28] The New Testament — Hebrews 8:13, 7:18—19, 10:9
[29] The New Testament — Hebrews 9:15—17
[30] S. Levine, *You take Jesus, I'll take God: How to refute Christian missionaries.* (Hamoroh Press, 1980)

Wouldn't it be peculiar if a king publicly issued a decree and proclaimed it to all of his people throughout the length and breadth of his realm and then a few years later, someone comes to the people and says that the king has told him personally that the first decree is now cancelled and that there's now a new decree and that the king had authorised him to tell everybody of this change and that the old law need no longer be obeyed? How would we view such a person? How would we view such a person especially if the king had told his people that he does not change his mind? And how should the people treat this individual when the king had warned his people that his law will never change? How should we view such a person if the king had warned his people to beware of anyone who comes to change his decree and that any such person should not be followed? Well, all three warnings are in the Torah!

There has never been any indication at all to the Jews that Jewish law would ever be annulled or changed for any other, ever.

2. Jesus did not fulfil the Messianic prophecies

An important question to address is, "What is the Messiah supposed to achieve?"

One of the main objectives of the real Messiah, as described in the Hebrew Scriptures and Jewish tradition is that he is to usher in an age of perfection typified by universal peace and recognition of the one God.[31]

The Jewish definition of the Messiah is based on the Hebrew Scriptures and tells that:

- The Messiah will build the Third Temple. *(Ezekiel 37:26-28)*.
- The Messiah will gather all Jews back to the Land of Israel. *(Isaiah 43:5-6)*.
- The Messiah's arrival will bring about an era of world peace, and end all hatred and suffering. *(Isaiah 2:4)*.
- The Messiah will spread universal knowledge of God and bring all humanity under the umbrella of ethical monotheism. *(Zechariah 14:9)*.
- The Messiah will bring about an end to all forms of idolatry. *(Zechariah 13:2)*.
- The Messiah's arrival will lead to end of the incidence of death. *(Isaiah 25:8)*.
- The Messiah's arrival will lead to the resurrection of the dead. *(Isaiah 26:19, 43:5-6; Daniel 12:2; Ezekiel 37:12-13)*.
- The Messiah's arrival will lead to each Tribe of Israel receiving and settling their tribal portion in the Land of Israel. *(Ezekiel 47:13-13)*.
- The Messiah's arrival will cause the river Nile to run dry. *(Isaiah 11:15)*.

---

[31] The Book of Prophets — Isaiah 2:1—4, 32:15—18, 60:15—18; Zephaniah 3:9; Hosea 2:20—22; Amos 9:13—15; Micah 4:1—4; Zechariah 8:23, 14:9; Jeremiah 31:33—34

All of the changes above are derived from the Hebrew Scriptures, and if any of these conditions are not met by the one who claims to be the Messiah, then he clearly is not the Messiah.

It is important to note that all of the above changes are observable. When they happen, everyone will be able to see that they have happened. There is very little room for wishy-washy "interpretation" or merely symbolic meaning. On the other hand, the changes that Christians claim were made by Jesus are **not** observable at all. The changes made by the Messiah according to Judaism will be certifiable, whereas the changes made by the Messiah according to Christianity can only be understood as a matter of faith. Today, even Christians recognise and admit that the changes that the real Messiah will make, promised by the Hebrew Scriptures and Jewish tradition, have not yet happened, so much so that they've suggested that Jesus will fulfil these unfulfilled promises in a "Second Coming". Yet there is no mention or indication of a "Second Coming" anywhere in the Hebrew Scriptures, and Judaism has always held that the Messiah will fulfil the prophecies outright.

The Christian claim that Jesus was the earthly human form of God is totally contradictory to what the Hebrew Scriptures state explicitly and unequivocally: *"God is not human,"* [32] and God does not have *"any likeness of anything physical."* [33]

---

[32] The Torah — Numbers 23:19; The Book of Prophets — Hosea 11:9
[33] The Torah — Deuteronomy 4:15—19

Another thing: It was never intended and God never commanded that the Messiah should ever be revered or worshipped as a physical form of God. His primary mission and accomplishment is to bring the world to peace and to teach to all its inhabitants the knowledge and awareness of the one God. Indeed, it can be argued that even Jesus himself never claimed divinity and that his statements about God as his "Father" were allegorical and not literal — something we see often in Hebrew Scriptures.[34]

3. Jesus did not fit the criteria of being the Messiah

The Hebrew Scriptures describe certain characteristics of the Messiah. Jesus of Nazareth did not meet many of these criteria.

The Messiah's Family Lineage

The Hebrew Scriptures speak of the Messiah as being the descendant of King David, from his father's side[35], who will rule Israel during an era of perfection.[36]

The Christian claim is that Jesus was the product of a virgin birth and had no biological father. Therefore, Jesus does not fulfil the Messianic requirement of being descended on his father's side from King David.

---

[34] The Book of Prophets — Daniel 17:3
[35] The Torah — Genesis 49:10; The Book of Prophets — Isaiah 11:1, Jeremiah 23:5, 33:17; Ezekiel 34:23—24, Hosea 3:4—5
[36] The Book of Prophets — Isaiah 11:1—9; Jeremiah 23:5—6, 30:7—10, 33:14—16; Ezekiel 34:11—31, 37:21—28; Hosea 3:4—5

Additionally, the Messiah must not only be a descendant of King David, but also of his son King Solomon.[37]   But according to the Christian New Testament[38], Jesus was not a descendant of Solomon, but of Solomon's half-brother Nathan.   Therefore Jesus was not a descendant of King David through King Solomon, and fails this test as well.

According to Jewish tradition, the Messiah will be born of human parents and possess normal physical attributes like other people. He will not be a demigod[39], and even though he will be able to perform miracles, he will not be a supernatural being.

It is also important to note that the Messiah may not be a descendant of Jehoiakim, Jechoniah, or Shealtiel, because this royal line was cursed.[40] However, the Christian New Testament states that Jesus was a descendant of Shealtiel.[41]

Hence Jesus' lineage does not accord with the received tradition and scriptural description of the expected lineage of the Messiah.

Time of the Messiah's Arrival

Comparing the time when Jesus lived, it is evident that Jesus did not live at the time described in the Hebrew

---

[37] The Book of Prophets — 2 Samuel 7:12—17; The Writings — 1 Chronicles 22:9—10

[38] The New Testament — Luke 3:31

[39] The Torah — Numbers 23:19, which states *"God is not a mortal"*.

[40] The Writings — 1 Chronicles 3:15—17; The Book of Prophets — Jeremiah 22:18—30

Scriptures regarding the arrival of the Messiah. Hebrew Scripture describes *"the latter days"* of the world as the time when the Temple will be established for the entire world to see[42], it will be a time when all the nations of the world will be judged by God[43], and when a great Jewish war would occur.[44]

Hence we see clearly that the prophets of the Hebrew Scriptures predicted that the coming of the true Messiah would happen at the *"latter days"* and not before — which was when Jesus of Nazareth lived.

Actions of the Messiah

Many of Jesus' actions contradicted those that are expected from the Messiah:

- We read in the Hebrew Scriptures that the Messiah will be a man of peace who will preach peace to the people.[45] Yet we read in the Christian New Testament that Jesus *"came not to bring peace but to bring the sword."*[46]

- We read in the Hebrew Scriptures that upon the arrival of the Messiah, *"the hearts of the fathers will turn to their children, and the hearts of the children will turn to their fathers."*[47] However, we read in the

---

[41] The New Testament — Matthew 1:11—12; Luke 3:27
[42] The Book of Prophets — Isaiah 2:2
[43] The Book of Prophets — Isaiah 2:4
[44] The Book of Prophets — Ezekiel 38:8
[45] The Book of Prophets — Zechariah 9:10
[46] The New Testament — Matthew 10:34
[47] The Book of Prophets — Malachi 4:6

Christian New Testament that Jesus has come *"to put father and son at variance."* [48]

- The Hebrew Scriptures tell that the Messiah will be served by *"all nations"* [49] and *"all rulers."* [50] Yet in the Christian New Testament, Jesus stated, concerning himself, that *"he has not come to be served by the son of man, but to serve others."* [51]

4. Verses in Hebrew Scriptures said to refer to Jesus are mistranslations

Verses in Hebrew Scripture can only be accurately comprehended and appreciated by someone who has a proper understanding of the Hebrew language and text. To understand an original text properly and correctly, it is just not enough to be merely conversant with translations made centuries later by people who often obtained their knowledge from a translation of a translation. Below are just some examples of these mistranslations and misinterpretations.

"The Virgin Birth"

The Christian idea of a virgin birth is due to a mistranslation of a verse in the Hebrew Scriptures, which describes an "almah" giving birth. [52] Even though both

---

[48] The New Testament — Matthew 10:35
[49] The Writings — Psalm 72:11
[50] The Writings — Daniel 7:27
[51] The New Testament — Matthew 20:28
[52] The Book of Prophets — Isaiah 7:14

Jewish and non-Jewish biblical scholars[53] state that the word "almah" has always meant nothing other than "a young woman" and has nothing to do with virginity, Christian scholars and interpreters down the centuries have persisted in translating the word "almah" as "virgin."

What is noteworthy, however, is that this Christian account of Jesus' birth is exactly the same as was commonly said by the pagans of the 1st century concerning how their pagan gods came about, namely, that mortal women were impregnated by the gods.[54]

"The Suffering Servant"

One of the most misquoted passages by Christians is a verse in the Hebrew Scriptures which they purport to show is a prophecy of the future emerging of Jesus, supposedly identifying him as the *"suffering servant"*.[55] However, the chapter in question directly follows the theme of the previous chapter, which describes the future exile and redemption of the Jewish People. The prophecies in these verses are written in the singular form because the Jews are collectively known as "Israel" and are invariably spoken of as a single national body. This is something that is quite common throughout

---

[53] M.A. Sweeney, *Isaiah 1—39: with an introduction to prophetic literature.* (Eerdmans, 1996)

[54] The legendary founder of Athens, *Theseus,* was said to be impregnated by the seed of both a mortal and a god. Read the book cited in **Footnote 30** for a thorough analysis of the similarities between Christianity and 1st century pagan religion.

[55] The Book of Prophets — Isaiah 53

Hebrew Scripture.[56] A clear example of this is found in Isaiah itself, where there is mention of Israel *"the servant of God"* more than ten times.[57]

The passage goes on to say that this *"suffering servant"* was *"oppressed and afflicted, yet he did not open his mouth; he was led like lamb to the slaughter".*[58] As a matter of fact, this excerpt could very well be an apt description of the Jewish People at the hands of many cruel leaders and nations throughout the ages. Indeed, these prophecies about the persecution of the Jewish People at the hands of the nations of the world are similar to the descriptions found elsewhere in Hebrew Scripture.[59]

But besides the plain misinterpretation, the literal text itself cannot be referring to Jesus simply because it doesn't fit the facts as reported elsewhere in the New Testament itself. The New Testament tells how when Jesus was being crucified by the Romans, not only was he not silent, but he even seemed to be blaspheming.[60] This is certainly not *"the silent lamb"* who *"did not open his mouth"* in the ordeal of his death. (Although countless Jews, suffering grisly deaths at the hands of people who attempted to wipe their nation out, did indeed suffer in silence and, not only did they not

---

[56] The Torah — Exodus 18:13, 19:2

[57] The Book of Prophets — Isaiah 43:8, 49:3

[58] The Book of Prophets — Isaiah 53:7

[59] The Writings — Psalm 44:11; The Book of Prophets — Jeremiah 12:3

[60] In the New Testament, Matthew 27:46, Jesus publicly cries out *"My God, my God, why hast Thou forsaken me?"*

blaspheme, but they even sanctified God by not surrendering to their cruel tormentors and renounce their faith.)

This chapter in Isaiah concludes that when the Jewish People are redeemed, the nations will recognise and accept responsibility for the terrible suffering and cruel deaths that they inflicted on the Jews. Clearly from the context, this chapter does not refer to Jesus but to the time of the redemption of the Jewish People.

5. Jewish belief is based upon National Revelation

As the Torah clearly points out, the entire nation was present when God revealed Himself to the Israelites at Mount Sinai.[61] In stark contrast, Christianity is predicated upon the prophetic claims of a single individual — Jesus of Nazareth (see **Chapter 2**).

•

The biggest challenge for Jews is the teachings of the Christian Scriptures. Christianity claims that Torah law has been abolished and is no longer valid. For Jews who follow the Torah with all their heart, these claims are unacceptable as the Torah itself says that it is eternal. Historically, this has caused distance between some Christians and Jews. My hope is that this gap can be bridged by a better understanding of the individual role that each of these religions have in this world.

---

[61] The Torah — Exodus 19

5 - ISLAM & MUHAMMAD

What is Islam and who was Muhammad?

Islam is a monotheistic religion that rapidly emerged in the 7th Century CE. It is based on the life and teachings of Muhammad ibn Abd-Allah, a merchant who lived in Mecca, Saudi Arabia. Although Islam and its holy scriptures only arrived on the world scene over two thousand years after Judaism did, Muslim tradition holds that Islam is a faith that has always existed and that it was progressively revealed to humanity by a number of previous prophets[1], with the final and complete revelation of the faith made through the prophet Muhammad. The result of this view is that the scriptures given by the previous prophets, including the Hebrew Scriptures, are also deemed by Islam to be authentic and legitimate scriptures from God.[2]

The holy scripture of Islam, "the Quran," describes how Muhammad, meditating in a cave on Mount Hira, was visited by the angel Gabriel, who commanded him to recite words which Muhammad perceived were the words of God.[3] These revelations continued for a number of years and were later recorded. The collection of traditions containing the sayings and actions of Muhammad is called the "Hadith."

---

[1] The Quran — 42:13, 3:67
[2] The Quran — 2:136, 3:3—4, 4:54, 5:12, 5:48, 10:37, 10:94, 29:46, 32:23
[3] The Quran — 81:19—29, 96:1—19

What is the Islamic position on Judaism?

Islam considers Judaism as an inherently God-given religion. The Jews are referred to in the Quran variously as "Jews," "Israelites," and "Children of Israel,"[4] but are also famously referred to as "the People of the Book"[5] with whom God chose to enter into a covenant.[6]

The Quran acknowledges the Hebrew Scriptures and even claims that there are predictions of Muhammad's prophecy in them.[7] Many prophets of the Hebrew Scriptures are declared by the Quran to be true messengers of God. As well as asserting that Muslims and Jews worship the same God[8], the Quran has been interpreted as stating that God assigned the land of Israel to the Jewish People.[9]

The influence of Judaism on Islam is evident as we can see how Muhammad based many of his beliefs and practices on those of the local Jewish population in his hometown. For example, the Muslim practices of not eating pig, of male circumcision, fasting during the first

---

[4] The Quran and Hadith make a distinction between these names, with the difference reflecting the history of the terms. The names 'Israelite' and 'Children of Israel' refer to the original, Biblical ancestors of the later 'Jews.' Generally speaking, the terms all refer to the same people — the nation which sprang from Abraham through Isaac and Jacob.

[5] The Quran — 3:64, 3:71, 3:187, 5:59

[6] The Quran — 2:40, 2:47, 2:63—65, 2:83—87, 2:122, 3:187, 5:12, 5:20, 5:70

[7] The Quran — 7:157

[8] The Quran — 29:46

[9] The Quran — 5:21, 17:104 (See the commentary in *Tafsir al-Tabari* by Abu Ja'far Muhammad ibn Jarir al-Tabari regarding Quran 5:21).

month of the year, and daily prayer with prostration (bowing down on one's knees)[10] were all direct influences from Judaism. Muslims originally even used to pray facing towards Jerusalem[11], the same direction that Jews around the world have been praying towards for over thirty three centuries.

There are many narratives and many ideas in the Quran that are similar to those in the Hebrew Scriptures. There is also much text and narrative material in the Quran that are almost identical to those found in earlier Jewish texts such as the Jewish Talmud.[12]

The Quran claims that Jews have been irresponsible with their revelations and that the words of God in the Hebrew Scriptures have been corrupted ("tahrif")[13], with Islamic scholars debating whether this corruption is textual[14] or is in its interpretation.[15] This accusation that the Jewish People have corrupted their Scriptures is in fact a response to the inconsistency that there is

---

[10] It was generally the norm amongst Jewish communities prior and during the emergence of Islam to bow down on ones knees during prayer, a sight that today is most commonly recognised as Islamic. Certain Jewish communities around the world, including Rambamist Jews ('Dor Daim') and Karaite Jews, continue this tradition until today. Most Jews today, however, reserve this practice only for certain prayers during the festivals of Rosh HaShanah and Yom Kippur.

[11] T. Mayer, S.A. Mourad, *Jerusalem: idea and reality*. (Routledge, 2008), pg. 87

[12] The Quran — 2:93, 5:27—32

[13] The Quran — 2:159, 2:75—79, 3:72—80, 3:78—79, 3:187, 4:155, 4:46, 5:13, 5:41, 6:91

[14] Al-Muqaddasi, Ibn Hazm, al-Biruni

[15] Ibn al-Layth, Ibn Rabban, Ibn Qutayba, al-Ya'qubi, al-Tabari, al-Baqillani, al-Ma'sudi

between the Quran and the earlier Hebrew Scriptures. All this seems to be in dispute with the Quran's often repeated statement[16] that it is impossible for anybody to change or corrupt the words of God. Islamic teachings affirm that Islamic law ("Shariah") was thus introduced to "perfect" and supersede the law of previous sacred scripture such as the Hebrew Scriptures.[17] In addition, the persistent refusal by the Jewish People to accept the Islamic revelation, renders them as "disbelievers" ("kufr").[18]

The Quran states[19] that the religious community of Islam ("ummah") is *the best community that has been brought forth for humanity,"* but only as long as its members would *"command what is right and forbid what is wrong, and believe in God."* The Quran does not elaborate on these requirements clearly. The question therefore arises: Is it permissible for Jews (and other "disbelievers") to *"command what is right and forbid what is wrong"* within their own religious traditions? Some verses in the Islamic scriptures say yes[20], others unequivocally say no.[21] Thus, the Quran can be used to

---

[16] The Quran — 6:34, 6:115, 10:64, 18:27

[17] The Quran — 2:106, 5:3, 5:48, 9:33

[18] The Quran — 5:44

[19] The Quran — 3:110

[20] The Quran — 2:62, 2:82, 2:113, 5:48, 5:69, 22:17

[21] The Quran — 2:20—24, 2:39, 2:90, 3:10, 3:19, 3:85, 3:181, 4:56, 4:161, 5:10, 5:51, 7:40, 9:29, 21:98, 48:13, 66:9, 98:6; The Hadith — Sahih Muslim, Book 1, Hadith 0284. Most traditional Islamic interpreter's state that these hostile verses abrogate the more welcoming verses cited in **Footnote 20** (see R. Firestone, *Jihad: The Origin of Holy War in Islam* (New York: Oxford University Press, 1999), pg. 48—65, 156).

justify either tolerance for Jews and others who do not believe in the Islamic revelation, or hostility towards these disbelievers, with the status of these disbelievers within Islam somewhat ambivalent.

What is the Jewish position on Islam?

Jewish sources make a clear distinction between the religious practice of Islam on the one hand and its belief and firm conviction in the one God on the other. Maimonides, arguably the greatest Jewish Authority on Islam, reflects his own view and the general view among other Jewish jurists[22] when he asserts that although it is an act of heresy for a Jew to become a Muslim, nevertheless Islam is intrinsically a monotheistic religion that shares much of the same foundations as Judaism.

Importantly, Islam is not considered idolatrous[23] unlike some major elements of Christianity which may be. This

---

[22] Ritva (Commentary on Talmud Pesachim 57a and Talmud Avodah Zarah 64b); Sefer Kolbo (Sefer Kolbo, Chapter 96); Ran (Responsa of the Ran, No. 5); R. Yeruham (Sefer Toldot Adam V'Hava, Netiv 17, Part 1, pg. 150, Tur 1); R. Karo (Bet Yosef, Yoreh De'ah 124:7); Radbaz (Responsa of the Radbaz, No. 344); Mahari Ben Lev (Responsa of Mahari Ben Lev, No. 1:118); Avnei Nezer (Responsa of Avnei Nezer, Yoreh De'ah 92); R. Ovadia Yosef (Responsa of Yabia Omer 7, Yoreh De'ah 12, Paragraph 4); Tashbetz (Responsa of Tashbetz, 1:14, 4:13); Maharitats (Responsa of Maharitats, 1:11); R. Moses Isserles (Responsa of Melamed Le'hoil, 2:55).

[23] Only a very few number of Jewish jurists label Islam an idolatrous religion (Responsa of Divre Yatsiv, Yoreh De'ah 40). There is another view that Islam is idolatrous only in certain aspects, and this prohibits Jews from entering a mosque only because it is a place where the Muslims publicly read and glorify portions of the Quran — and the Quran teaches that the Hebrew Scriptures are false and corrupted (Responsa of Tzitz Eliezer, 18:47).

difference will determine much of the interaction between Jews and Muslims.

The Jewish view of Islam as a non-idolatrous religion can be seen from the fact that Jews are permitted to pray in their mosques and that they may derive benefit from their wine — something that Jewish law has not always extended to Christianity.[24] Although Jews will not — and cannot — accept Islam as having authority over themselves, nevertheless Jews do consider many of Islam's teachings as acceptable for the rest of mankind, complying as they do with the Seven Noahide Laws.[25] These laws and their origins are briefly discussed in **Chapter 3** of this book.

Needless to say, Jews strongly refute the Islamic claim[13] that the Hebrew Scriptures have been changed or corrupted, since there is no proof of this nor any reason for it to have occurred. Furthermore, the oldest

---

[24] So as to prevent assimilation and handling objects of idolatry, Jewish law makes some constraints on foods and drinks that are produced by idolaters, and the original Christians were under this category. These restrictions are on foods commonly associated with religious ceremonies or have some religious significance (such as wine, bread and oil that were often offered to idols as libations or offered as a sacrifice to some idol or other as part of an idolaters' worship, or indeed were consumed as part of a religious ritual). Additionally, many Jewish Authorities forbade Jews from praying in churches that displayed images and sculptures of Jesus, as this was deemed as idolatry. Mosques, however, include no such things and are thus acceptable for a Jew to pray in.

[25] The Quran, in 15:87, refers to *"Seven Verses"* which may be a reference to the Seven Noahide Laws. Furthermore, the same laws found in the Seven Noahide Laws are explicitly mentioned and promoted in the Quran — 5:3, 17:22, 17:23, 17:32, 17:33, 17:34, 17:35.

discovered versions of the Hebrew Scriptures match the versions that are in use all over the world today.[26]

It is a common misconception that the Jewish People did not follow Muhammad as their prophet **only** due to the fact that he was not Jewish. This is an ignorant accusation because Jewish tradition states that there were actually seven non-Jewish prophets.[27]

Jewish tradition holds that while Abraham's son Isaac is the forefather of the Jewish People, the Islamic line is descended from another son of Abraham, Ishmael.

Maimonides states that the prevalence of Islam in the world is part of God's plan to disseminate monotheism throughout the world together with the morals and values of the Hebrew Scriptures and thus to prepare mankind for the Messianic era.[28]

There are four main reasons as to why Jewish authorities did not accept Islam as a replacement to Judaism:

1. *Aspects of the Quran dispute the Hebrew Scriptures*
2. *Jesus' status in Islam as the Messiah & future prophecy*
3. *Verses in Hebrew Scriptures said to refer to Muhammad are mistranslations*
4. *Jewish belief is based upon National Revelation*

---

[26] Garry K. Brantley, *The Dead Sea Scrolls and Biblical Integrity. Reason & Revelation.* (Apologetics Press, 1995), 15:4, pg. 25–30
[27] The Talmud — Baba Bathra 15b
[28] Moses Maimonides, *Mishneh Torah.* Hilkhot Melakhim 11:10—12

1. Aspects of the Quran dispute the Hebrew Scriptures

There are many narratives from the Hebrew Scriptures that are referred to or are retold in the Quran — which was compiled two thousand years after those Hebrew Scriptures — but in versions that seem to dispute the Hebrew Scriptures.

Here are just a few examples out of many others:

- In the Quran, one of Noah's sons rejects him, refuses to board the Ark and consequently dies in the great flood.[29] In the Torah, all three of Noah's sons and their wives join him and board the Ark.[30]

- In the account of Abraham preparing his son for sacrifice, the Quran does not specifically mention the name of the son[31] but the majority Islamic opinion is that Ishmael was the son that Abraham was commanded by God to offer up as a sacrifice.[32] The Torah, on the other hand, repeatedly states that it

---

[29] The Quran — 11:43
[30] The Torah — Genesis 7:13
[31] The Quran — 37:99—113. It is important to note that in the Quran's account, directly after the aborted sacrifice of Isaac, Abraham is told of the coming of Isaac's birth and thus, according to the Quran, it must be Ishmael who was about to be sacrificed as Isaac had not been born yet.
[32] R. Firestone, *Journeys in holy lands: the evolution of the Abraham—Ishmael legends in Islamic exegesis.* (State University of NY Press, 1990), pg. 135

was his other son, Isaac[33], born from Sarah, who was to be the sacrifice.

- The Quran states that Ishmael was a prophet, but the Hebrew Scriptures do not impute to Ishmael any prophetic status at all.[34]

- The Quran refers to Abraham's father as "Azar"[35] whereas in the Torah his name is "Terah."[36]

- The Quranic version[37] of the account of Moses meeting his wife is significantly different to the original version described in the Torah.[38]

- The Quran claims that Pharoah's wife adopted Moses[39] even though the Torah says clearly that it was Pharoah's daughter who adopted him.[40]

- The Quran says that God punished the Egyptians with nine plagues[41] whereas the Torah speaks of the Ten Plagues of Egypt and describes them at great length.[42]

- In its own version of the Exodus, the Quran states that Haman was a counselor in Pharaoh's court[43] at

---

[33] The Torah — Genesis 22:5—8
[34] The Quran — 2:136, 19:54
[35] The Quran — 6:74
[36] The Torah — Genesis 11:26
[37] The Quran — 28:23—28
[38] The Torah — Exodus 2:15—22
[39] The Quran — 28:7—9
[40] The Torah — Exodus 2:1—10
[41] The Quran — 17:101—103, 27:12—13
[42] The Torah — Exodus 7:14—12:36
[43] The Quran — 28:6, 28:8, 28:38, 29:39, 40:24, 40:36

the time of the Exodus whereas in fact, of course, Haman is the central figure and the principal antagonist in the plan to wipe out all the Jews throughout the Empire of the Persian king Ahasuerus as is clearly recorded in the Book of Esther, compiled more than a thousand years after the Exodus.

- The Quran states that Lot was a prophet[44] but the Hebrew Scriptures do not impute to Lot any prophetic status at all.

- The Quran, astonishingly, claims that Jews regarded the Prophet Ezra as *"the Son of God"* [45] — a term that is anathema to the Jews and in any case untrue.

- The Quran does not accept the whole body of law concerning animal sacrifices and atonement that are expounded upon at length and referred to throughout the Hebrew Scriptures.

Jews throughout the centuries have found it difficult to reconcile these differences, especially when according to Islam, both the Hebrew Scriptures and the Quran are from the same God. The Jewish People have been unable to accept this seemingly altered version of their history and have never been able to take Islam as its successor, especially as the Torah repeatedly states that its teachings and laws are eternal.[46] Nevertheless, a concerted effort should be made by Jews and Muslims,

---

[44] The Quran — 7:80—84, 15:67—77, 26:160—168, 29:28—31
[45] The Quran — 9:30
[46] The Torah — Deuteronomy 13:1, 29:28, 33:4; Leviticus 23:14

at all levels, to primarily focus on the morals of each historical narrative – not necessarily the differences.

2. Jesus' status in Islam as the Messiah & future prophecy

God communicated to people through prophecy for nearly the entire Biblical period, from the prophet Adam until the prophet Malachi. At the time of Muhammad's arrival, and even today, other than Elijah as the bringer of the good news of the imminent redemption and the coming of the Messiah[47], the Jews do not await the coming of any prophet. Many individuals claiming to be the Messiah have been and gone, including Jesus of Nazareth (whose followers later formed what is known today as Christianity).

However, as has been discussed, the Jewish Authorities and leaders of the time found that the Messianic claims of Jesus of Nazareth were false and they utterly rejected him. When then Muhammad, who came six hundred years later, taught that Jesus was the Messiah prophesised in the Hebrew Scriptures[48], the Jewish Authorities saw this as going against what the Hebrew Scriptures taught about the Messiah.

In addition, Judaism teaches that no prophet other than Elijah can exist after the death of the prophet Malachi[49],

---

[47] The Book of Prophets — Malachi 3:1, 3:23, 4:5
[48] The Quran — 3:45—46, 4:172—173, 5:76, 9:31
[49] The Talmud — Baba Bathra 12a-b; Sotah 48b; Yoma 9b; Sanhedrin 11a-b

and the death of Malachi occurred almost one thousand years before Mohammed was even born.

The Jewish People at the time of Muhammad were certain that Muhammad was not Elijah, nor even a reincarnation of Elijah, for a number of reasons:

- As mentioned above repeatedly, Judaism rejects the claim that Jesus of Nazareth is the Messiah and has clear proof that he was not, yet Muhammad believed that he was.

- The prophet Elijah will precede the Messiah and will herald his imminent arrival. Muhammad lived six hundred years after Jesus. Since Muhammad considered Jesus to be the Messiah, that meant that the Messiah had come six hundred years before the herald who was to announce his coming!

3. Verses in Hebrew Scriptures said to refer to Muhammad are mistranslations

As abovementioned, the Quran states that Muhammad and his future prophecy have been referred to in the Hebrew and Christian Scriptures that existed long before Muhammad's arrival on the world scene.

Some Islamic scholars have analysed the Hebrew and Christian Scriptures to try and find which verses these may be.[50] However, many Jews and Christians state that

---

[50] C. Adang, *Muslim Writers on Judaism and the Hebrew Bible from Ibn Rabban to Ibn Hazm.* (Leiden, New York, Cologne: E.J. Brill, 1996)

these verses said to refer to Muhammad are merely mistranslations or misinterpretations taken out of context. We will now look at a few examples.

"A prophet like Moses"

Some Muslims claim that the Torah foretells Muhammad's prophecy in the following verse:

"I will raise up for them a prophet like him (Moses) from among their brothers;

I will put my words in his mouth, and he will tell them everything that I command him."

- The Torah, Deuteronomy 18:18

Muslims claim that this is referring to Muhammad and since Muhammad is a descendant of Abraham's other son, Ishmael, he thus qualifies as the "brother" referred to in this verse. However, it is very clear from other verses in this chapter of the Torah[51] that the meaning of the word "brother" is a fellow Israelite, not a non-Israelite such as Muhammad. Furthermore, other descendants of Abraham, through his other children, are mentioned often in the Torah but they are never referred to as the "brothers" of the Israelites.

It is also manifestly clear from the above verse that the future prophet described would be "like Moses." We thus need to identify the crucial attributes that the future prophet would have to possess to be considered "like Moses" and these are laid out in the Torah.[52]

---

[51] The Torah — Deuteronomy 17:15
[52] The Torah — Deuteronomy 34:10—12

1. This future prophet is to speak the words that God puts in his mouth, *as did Moses.*
2. This future prophet would speak with God, *as did Moses.*
3. This future prophet would perform miracles, signs and wonders, *as did Moses.*

Muhammad said that he heard the Quran from someone he believed to be the angel Gabriel, and Muhammad repeated the words that this angel spoke.[53] This does not meet the first and second requirements of the verse since he received his revelation through a medium — as he said, the angel Gabriel — and did not hear from God directly. Additionally, the Quran states that Muhammad performed no miracles[54], which the Quran itself highlights as a reason why certain people living at the time did not believe his claims.[55] This means that, according to many Jews and Christians, Muhammad did not comply with the third and final requirement to be the individual alluded to in the specific verse above.

The Song of Songs

The Song of Songs is a love poem and is in the third section of the Hebrew Scriptures, "The Writings." It was composed by King Solomon and is an allegory which describes the love of God for the Jewish People and their love for Him in a beautiful parable of a married couple yearning for each other.

---

[53] The Quran — 53:2—5
[54] The Quran — 6:57—58
[55] The Quran — 28:48

Some Muslims believe that a verse in this poem refers to Muhammad:

*"His mouth is most sweet: he is **altogether lovely**.*
This is my beloved, and this is my friend, O daughters of
Jerusalem."

- The Writings, The Song of Songs 5:16

The words **"altogether lovely"** in the verse are pronounced as "machmaddim" in Hebrew. This, Muslims claim, is a reference to Muhammad as the word "machmad" (which is the singular of "machmaddim") sounds similar to the name "Muhammad."

In the context of the passage the person described as "machmad" ('delightful', 'precious') in this allegorical portrayal by Solomon[56] and who is loved by a Shulamite[57], is auburn-haired[58] and this description does not fit Muhammad. Furthermore, it would have been quite meaningless to his audience for Solomon to use in his poem someone who not only was not contemporaneous with his audience but indeed was to live only two thousand years later.

Generally in the Hebrew Scriptures, the word "machmad" means something desirable. The word is derived from the root "chamad" which means 'desire.'

If we were to accept that the word "machmad" refers to Muhammad, then we should look at all the occurrences of that word in Hebrew Scripture. Other verses in the

---

[56] The Writings — Song of Songs 3:11
[57] The Writings — Song of Songs 6:13. A Shulamite is someone from a region today known as Sulem in north-eastern Israel.
[58] The Writings — Song of Songs 5:10

Hebrew Scriptures state that "machmad" was to be destroyed[59], that "machmad" has been kidnapped by an enemy[60], that "machmad" has been traded for food[61], that "machmad" has been slaughtered by God[62], that "machmad" has been removed by God[63], that "machmad" is to be profaned by God[64], and is to be buried in nettles[65] and will be carried away by pagans into their temples.[66] Of course, Muslims would consider it blasphemous if a Muslim was to ever attribute any of these things to their prophet Muhammad. Thus, it may be difficult to associate the word "machmad" in the Hebrew Scriptures with "Muhammad", the prophet of Islam.

4. Jewish Belief is Based upon National Revelation

Like Christianity, the Islamic religion is predicated upon the prophetic claims of a single individual — Muhammad — as opposed to God revealing Himself to the entire nation, like what happened at Mount Sinai at the initiation of Judaism.

Furthermore, the Torah explains how God gave His laws directly to Moses in front of an entire nation, and that

---

[59] The Book of Prophets — Isaiah 64:10—11
[60] The Writings — Lamentations 1:10
[61] The Writings — Lamentations 1:11
[62] The Writings — Lamentations 2:4; Hosea 9:16
[63] The Writings — Ezekiel 24:16
[64] The Writings — Ezekiel 24:21
[65] The Book of Prophets — Hosea 9:6
[66] The Book of Prophets — Joel 3:5

Moses wrote it down over the years as it was dictated to him — not in a vision and not through any mediation of an angel. This is in stark contrast with what Muslims traditionally believe about the Quran. Muslims believe that the Quran was given to Muhammad by God through the medium of the oral recitation of the Quran by the angel Gabriel. The Quran states that Muhammad was illiterate, that he could not read or write.[67] Consequently, the early followers of Muhammad recorded the revelations and sayings of Muhammad and eventually compiled them to form the Quran. **Chapter 2** of this book discusses this major difference between the beginnings of Judaism and Islam.

•

While Muslims and Jews may not agree on certain points, our religions share the same Abrahamic root. The traditional Islamic position views anyone who does not accept the laws of the Quran as a "disbeliever". The traditional Jewish position views proper Muslims as passionate believers dedicated to the one God. The important thing, from the Jewish point of view, is that we support and encourage each other. As the Quran states so eloquently,

"To each is a goal to which God turns him; then strive together towards all that is good.

Wheresoever you are, God will bring you together, for God has power over all things."

- The Quran, 2:148

---

[67] The Quran — 7:157

6 – EASTERN RELIGIONS

"Eastern religions" refers to religions originating in the Eastern world — India, China, Japan and Southeast Asia — all very different from Western religions. These Eastern religions, unlike the earlier ones discussed in previous chapters, are not part of Abraham's monotheistic mission, and are generally considered by Jewish sources as being idolatrous in nature.

There is an exception. The Eastern religion of Sikhism is monotheistic in nature and is not idolatrous and Jewish Authorities hold it to be similar to the other monotheistic religions discussed previously.

JUDAISM & IDOLATRY

The association between certain Eastern religions and idolatry is a critical determining factor of the Jewish position concerning them. There is a whole tractate in Jewish law dedicated to understanding and analysing what idolatry actually is and what interactions and connection Jews are permitted or forbidden to have with idol-worshippers.[1]

The Torah strongly condemns any form of idolatry.[2] Jewish law holds that idolatry is not only the worship of a statue, icon, picture or any such object but includes also even the worship of God through worshipping any

---

[1] The Talmud — Tractate Avodah Zarah
[2] The Torah — Exodus 20:2-3; Deuteronomy 7:25; Deuteronomy 5:6-7

purported mediators or any artifacts, man-made or naturally occurring, or worshipping any kind of representations of God. Some such representations are found within Eastern religions such as Hinduism and Buddhism.

As we have seen in **Chapter 4**, even in a so-called monotheistic religion such as Christianity there might very well be parts that are idolatrous. As we have seen, too, there are different opinions among Jewish Authorities as to whether or not apparently polytheistic religions need inevitably to be considered as idolatrous and forbidden if, together with their various gods, their adherents also acknowledge and worship the one God (an arrangement called "Shittuf," that is, "partnership").[3] It is also important to note that although Jewish law may not completely prohibit such partially idolatrous worship to non-Jews, nevertheless such worship is of course totally forbidden for Jews.

As will be discussed below, in Judaism there is no punishment in the courts of man for offences or crimes committed by thought alone. Idolaters are therefore only liable for punishment in the courts of law of man for their actions, not for their thoughts or beliefs.

Since Jewish Law has long attributed most Eastern religions with idol-worship, there is little discussion about these religions in the Jewish sources.

---

[3] "Shittuf": a Jewish legal term meaning a "partnership," that is, worshipping the one God but in association with other gods (see **Chapter 4** for a deeper look at this concept).

There is some discussion, however, concerning Hinduism and Buddhism.

What is the Jewish position on Hinduism?

According to a number of Jewish scholars[4], Hinduism is equal to idolatry. According to these Authorities, therefore, all the laws that apply to idolaters also apply to Hindus, *e.g.* a Jew is forbidden to derive benefit from Hindu objects of worship and other such limitations and sanctions. The great Jewish philosopher and codifier Maimonides[5] rules that the Hindus are considered a remnant of an ancient idolatrous community known as the Sabians, but he does not specifically state whether or not Hinduism itself is an acceptable religion permitted by the Noahide laws which are incumbent upon all non-Jews.

However, in 2008, a Hindu-Jewish interfaith summit called by the World Council of Religious Leaders took place in Jerusalem, Israel.[6] At this summit, a historic statement was issued to end the presumption that Hinduism is tantamount to idol-worship.

---

[4] R. Ezekiel Landau (Noda B'Yehudah, Tinyana, Orah Hayyim No. 10); R. Jacob ben Sheshet; R. Yehudah Moshe Ftayah
[5] Moses Maimonides, *The Guide For The Perplexed.* Volume 3, Chapter 29, pg. 515
[6] This summit took place on February 17—20th 2008 in Jerusalem, Israel. The Jewish delegation consisted of the American Jewish Association, the Chief Ashkenazi Rabbinate of Israel (Rabbi Yona Metzger), the President of Israel and various Chief Rabbis of other countries such as Turkey, Spain, and Belgium. The Hindu delegation consisted of members of the Hindu Dharma Acharya Sabha, including representatives of Shankaracharyas.

nent read:

> is recognised that One Supreme Being in its
> ıormless and manifest aspects has been
> worshipped by Hindus over millennia. The Hindu
> relates to only the One Supreme Being when he
> or she prays to a particular manifestation. This
> does not mean that Hindus worship 'idols.' They
> worship 'devataas,' who are manifestations of the
> One Supreme Being.

This is an important statement in that it makes it clear that Hindus believe in and worship *"One Supreme Being."* The statement has many ramifications, one of the most important being that Jewish law is now able to consider Hinduism the same as Christianity, namely, a religion whose worship incorporates "a partnership."[3]

Having said that, it must be borne in mind that even if Hindu **worship** may qualify as a "partnership," nevertheless Hindu **practice** may not. In other words, if Hinduism requires its adherents — or indeed only allows — certain acts that qualify as idolatrous, then there can be no leniency in the matter of Hindu worship, either.[7]

What is the Jewish Position on Buddhism?

Buddhism, in its rawest form as the non-theistic philosophy taught by Buddha, is mostly broadly compatible with Judaism. However, Buddhism as practiced by many peoples in many places takes the veneration of the Buddha and the various "enlightened

---

[7] Avnei Nezer, Yoreh De'ah 123:9—10

beings" ("bodhisattvas") to a level of veneration that is often indistinguishable from worship, and that is what makes it forbidden to Jews. Praying to such entities rather than to God is considered idolatry and is a key tenet of the most popular form of Buddhism today, Mahayana Buddhism. Additionally, the prevalent pantheism in Buddhism, that is, the veneration of a number of gods, is in direct contradiction to Judaism and the ideals taught in the Hebrew Scriptures.

Nevertheless, Buddhism has attracted many Jews in the past and present. Jokingly known as "JewBu's" or "BuJu's," these Jewish individuals turn to Buddhism as a way of attaining a transcendental state of consciousness ("nirvana") which allows them to exit the realm of this world. Judaism, on the other hand, is passionate about engaging with the world that we live in. The contrast between Buddhism and Judaism can hardly be greater. At the risk of over-simplification, it can be said that Buddhism seeks to elevate the mind and consciousness through divesting oneself of physicality whereas Judaism seeks not only to elevate one's mind and consciousness but to permeate all of one's body and every physical experience with sacredness and holiness, to elevate the whole of one's existence, to sanctify one's whole being, in the service of God. Judaism seeks not only to enlighten the mind but to also train the physical body, to sanctify it and to sanctify all life, by doing what God has commanded and by living our lives according to God's will.

There are many other differences between Buddhism and Judaism and one of the most fundamental is what each teaches concerning God. Buddhism has long denied or dismissed the idea of God in man's life[8], and at best has expressed ambivalence about God which removes God from human existence. Judaism, on the other hand, teaches that God is the source of all existence and the fulfilment of all mankind's striving. Buddhism finds the world to be ultimately purposeless, whereas the basis and foundation of Judaism is the recognition that all humans have a purpose in life.

IDOLATROUS BELIEF & IDOLATROUS PRACTICE

As briefly mentioned above, it is important to note that there is a difference between idolatrous **belief** and idolatrous **practice**, and the Hebrew Scriptures, too, keep them clearly separate. Thus, Judaism teaches that a person's idolatrous beliefs (*i.e.* that he believes in multiple deities) are not judged in the courts of man; only the immoral practices associated with such beliefs, for example, human sacrifice, ritual murder and acts which are abominations ("religious" or not) are judged in human courts. Punishments are mandated for those that actively worship an idol because, among other reasons, this worship is considered the start of committing the immoral and ruinous practices of idolatry. Idol-worship is forbidden not only because it itself is the opposite of Godliness but just as much because its associated

---

[8] Thanissaro Bhikku (1997), *Acintita Sutta: Unconjecturable.* AN 4.77 (translated from Pali into English)

immoral practices can be an automatic follow-on, all emanating from the corrosive lack of belief in the one God. All this is crucial in understanding the prohibition of idolatry and why this prohibition is commanded as one of the Seven Noahide Laws incumbent upon all mankind (see **Chapter 3**).

Despite the great chasm of contrast that exists between Judaism and the Eastern religions, the tolerance and ambivalence that exists between Judaism and these Eastern religions might be due to the fact that these religions have no real deity or power in the Western sense. It could be argued that these "religions" are nothing more than attempts at spirituality, mere experiments in discovering a philosophy for life, more than a way of worshipping God. That being so, if people are sincere in their quest for the Godly and the spiritual, if they genuinely observe and comply with the basic moral precepts as exemplified in the Seven Noahide Laws commanded by God, then Judaism would not consider them as idolaters.

7 – FINAL WORDS

The words[1] of Rabbi Israel Lipschitz (1782—1860), who is recognised as one of the finest commentators of the Mishnah[2], are a fitting conclusion to our discussion:

The Mishnah says, **"If there is no Torah there is no civilisation [or "way of the land"]."**

The word "Torah" here cannot be meant in the narrow sense of the Five Books of Moses since there are many ignorant people who have not learned it, and many pious among the non-Jews who do not keep the Torah, and yet they are ethical and follow the "way of the land," that is, they are truly civilised. Rather, the correct meaning seems to be as follows: Every people, every folk, every national group, has its own religion, each comprising three fundamental principles:

(1)   Belief in a revealed Torah or 'guide' ultimately originating from God;

(2)   Belief in reward and punishment, for God the Creator expects every creature to comply with His will; and

(3)   Belief in an afterlife, where the worthy will experience the blessed life that God intends for all good people.

They only disagree on the interpretation of these principles. These three principles are what this Mishnah calls "Torah."

This Jewish understanding offers a vision of pluralism based on a general acknowledgement of Divine

---

[1] Rabbi Israel Lipschitz. *Tiferet Yisrael.* Avot 3:17
[2] "Mishnah": An authoritative collection of exegetical material embodying the tradition of Jewish law and forming the first part of the "Talmud" (see **Glossary**).

Revelation, of reward and punishment and of an afterlife in a next world — three principles found in all great religions.

Rather than approaching different religions as an "other," Judaism stresses the common foundation of all humankind based on the moral principles communicated by God to all mankind. It is this which is the only true basis on which can be built the universal brotherhood of man.

·

This book set out to provide a summary of the reasons as to why Jews remained Jews and did not give in to later religions that attempted to convert them. My hope is that the reader now has a better understanding of the Jewish position, but can also appreciate the common thread that holds the great faiths of the world together.

Instead of attempting to convince others to abandon one's religion and join their own, the Jewish People are commanded to influence the world with morality and decency, regardless of who you are and what you believe.

I commend my brothers and sisters of different religions who do the same. I invite the rest of you to join us.

A WORD TO THE JEWISH STUDENT

Rabbi Osher Yitzchok Baddiel

London, England

You are a member of the Jewish People, God's Chosen People. There's no need for you to apologise for this or to be embarrassed about it. Being "chosen" doesn't mean you are a superior race. It means that you have a responsibility and a duty to the rest of mankind, to elevate them, to ennoble them, to introduce God and spirituality into their lives and their world, to make people happy, contented and fulfilled in their lives.

The Jewish way of life is called Judaism. Be proud and humble, in equal measure, of the fact that noble teachings of the major religions of the world are all derived from Judaism. Do not be surprised about this. It is as it should be. That's our job: the Jewish People have the duty and responsibility to teach about God in the world. That's why we are "chosen" and that's what "chosen" means.

Some people might try to get you to forsake your own People. Don't forsake your duty, your responsibility.

Remember: Judaism is the first monotheistic religion in the world. This is a historical fact. The beginnings of Judaism date back to almost two thousand years before any other.

God gave us His Torah, that is, the Hebrew Scriptures, together with the Oral Law, to be our instructions manual, to teach us how we are to live our lives and how we are to do our duty to others. In the Torah, God promises that He will never forsake us for anybody else and that he will never give another Torah to anybody else. He also says that anybody who comes and says different is a liar. Believe God. Even if missionaries may mean well, they are wrong to try to get you to desert your own People.

Remember how many Jews in the past have stood firm and not deserted their People even in the face of the most horrible torture and even death, and be proud to belong to this same

People. And consider carefully that Judaism must be worth quite something if so many people have been willing to give their lives for it.

Always strive to be an example of a good, loyal Jew, a person who lives in God's world and lawfully enjoys His blessings, a person who seeks and finds spiritual satisfaction and fulfilment through following God's Torah. Now go and learn that Torah!

Encourage others to improve their lives by bringing God into their lives. Encourage the Christian and the Muslim to live their lives according to the good teachings in their religions. They have no obligation at all to become Jews and you should rejoice in their happiness when they live their lives according to God's wishes for them.

In this way, each human being will merit God's blessings of happiness and spiritual fulfilment. Even if we are all different, at the same time we will be together in the common purpose of giving pleasure to God Almighty, Who has told us that nothing is more precious to Him than a happily united family of humankind.

Made in the USA
San Bernardino, CA
06 February 2014